TIKA
The Tiger

Written by KATHY QUIGLEY
Illustrated by FRANK RICCIO

PEQUOT PUBLISHING

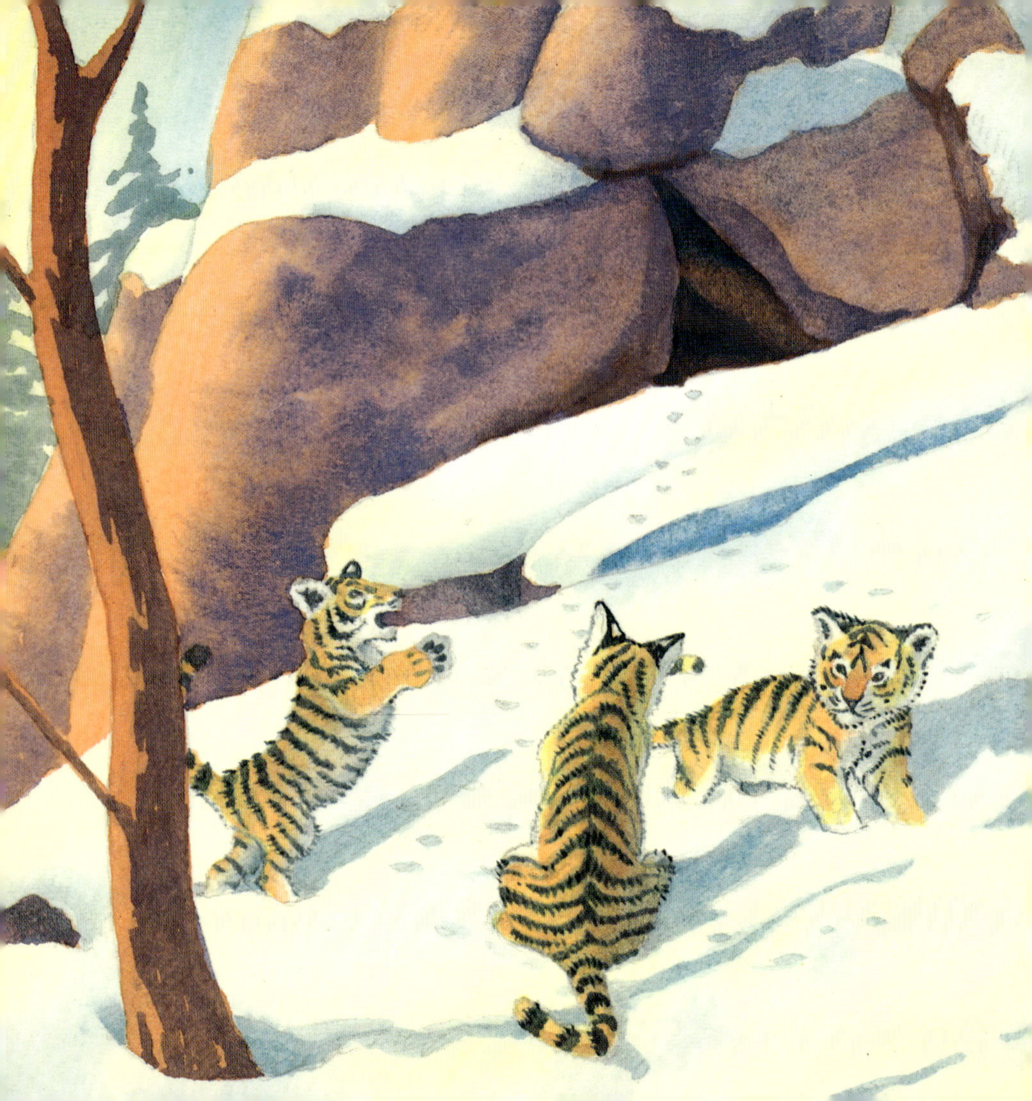

On a sunny, sparkly winter day, Tika and her brothers Sika and Mika were playing in the fresh snow. They are Siberian tiger cubs, and will live most of their lives in the snow.

Their mother Natasha had left them for the day while she went hunting for their dinner. She often did this. "Stay right here near the den," she always said. "You are too young to be in the forest alone."

Tika and Sika were playing hide-and-seek. The black stripes on their yellow coats matched the dark trunks of the trees, so hiding was easy. Silly little Mika was having fun chasing his tail, and echoing everything his brother and sister said.

Tika loved to explore and soon began to wander. "Tika, we are supposed to stay here and play," called Sika. "Stay here and play!" echoed Mika.

But Tika was busy following some fresh deer tracks in the snow. Before long she had strayed too far to hear Sika and Mika.

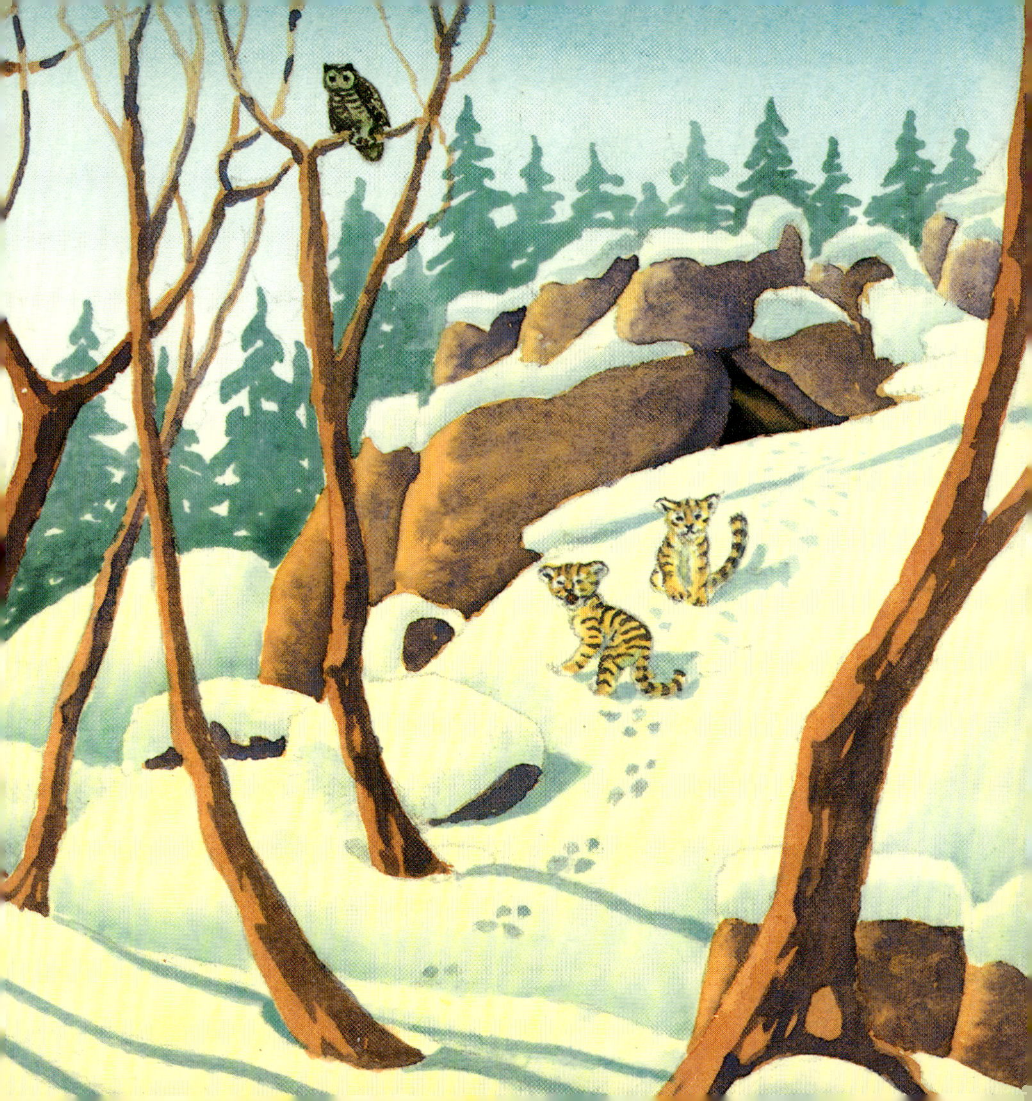

Tika was not worried. "I know the way home," she thought. But the more Tika walked, the more confused she became. All the trees looked the same! Nothing seemed familiar. "Sika! Sika!" she called hopefully. But she heard no answer.

Soon the warm sun set, and snow began to swirl in the crisp air. Although Tika's beautiful thick coat kept her warm, she was getting a little scared. She thought about her warm, safe den. She thought about Sika, Mika, and especially her mother.

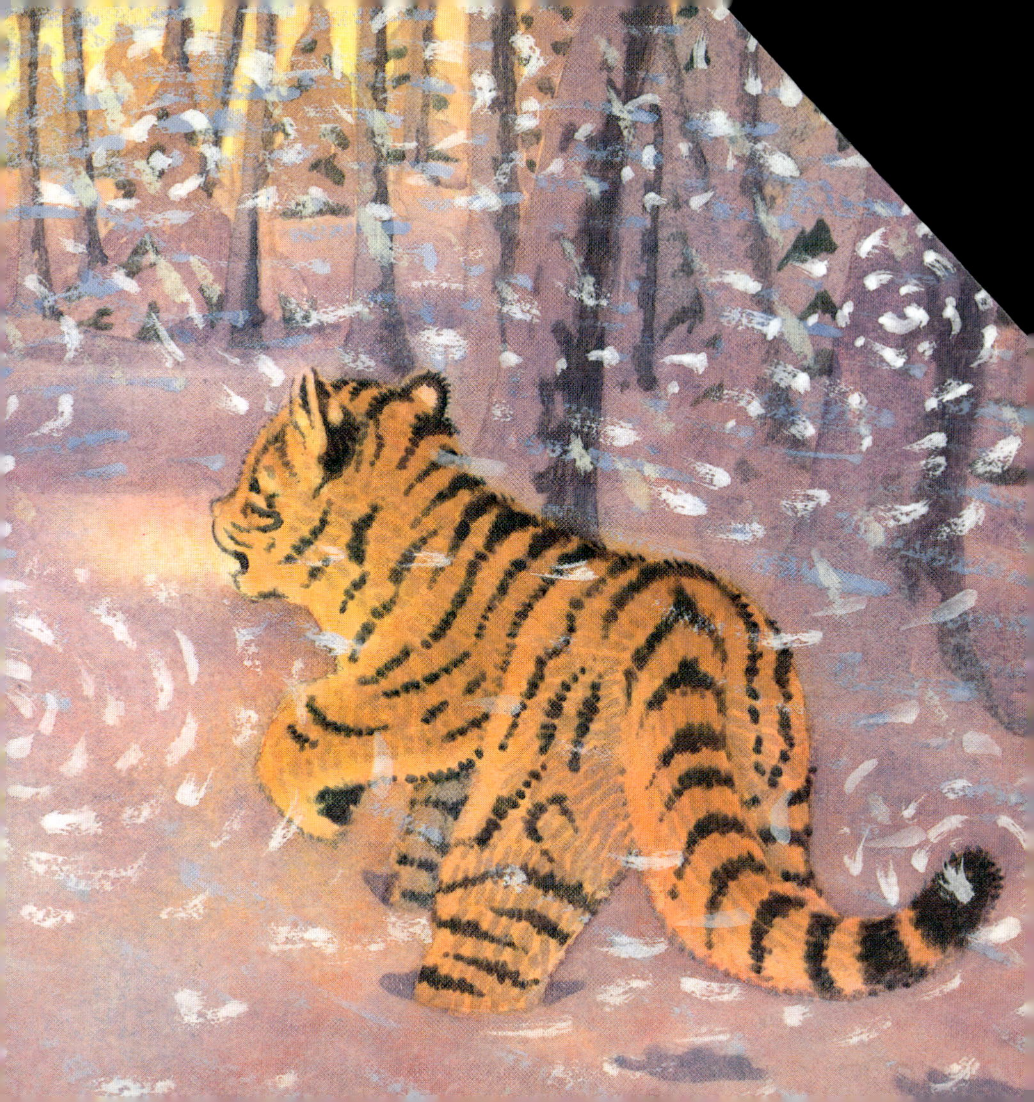

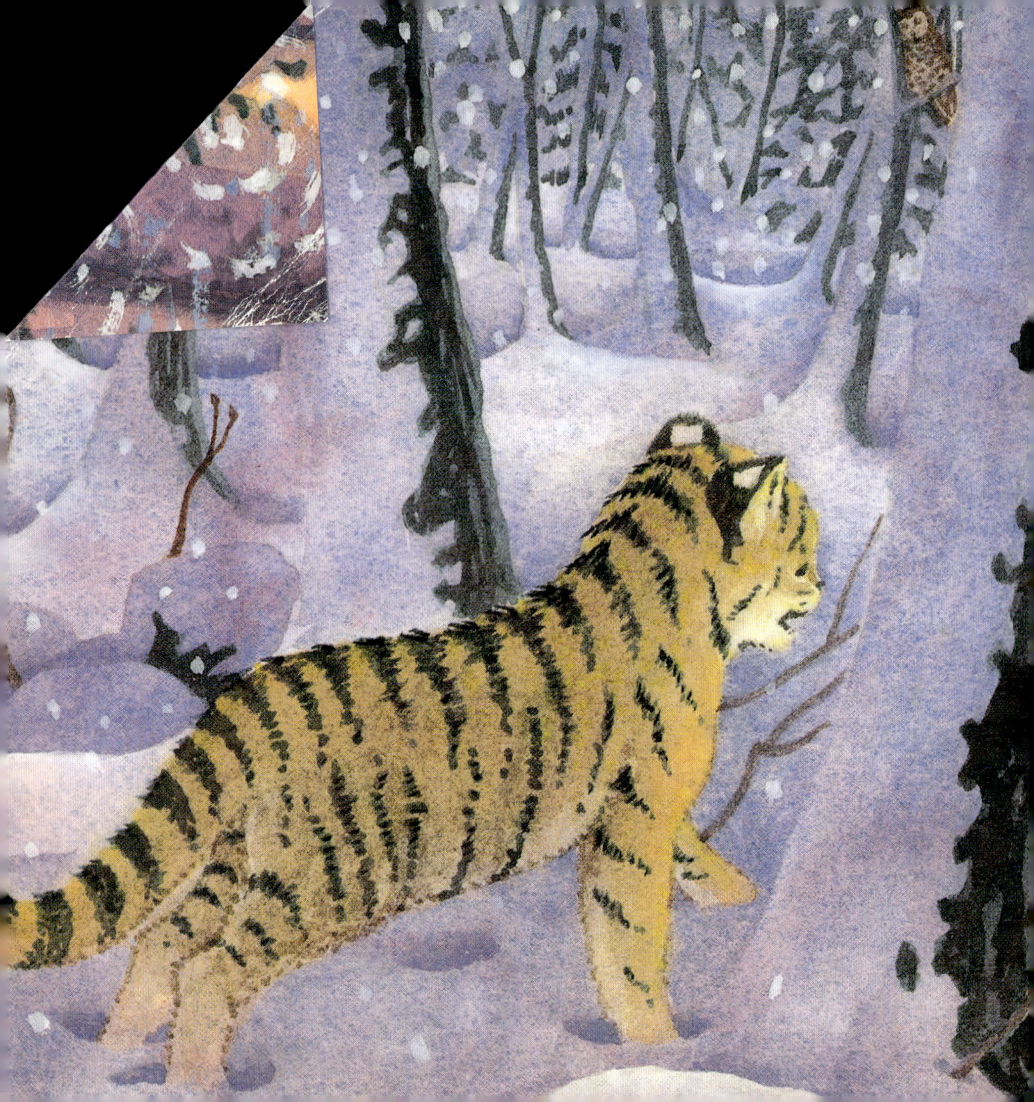

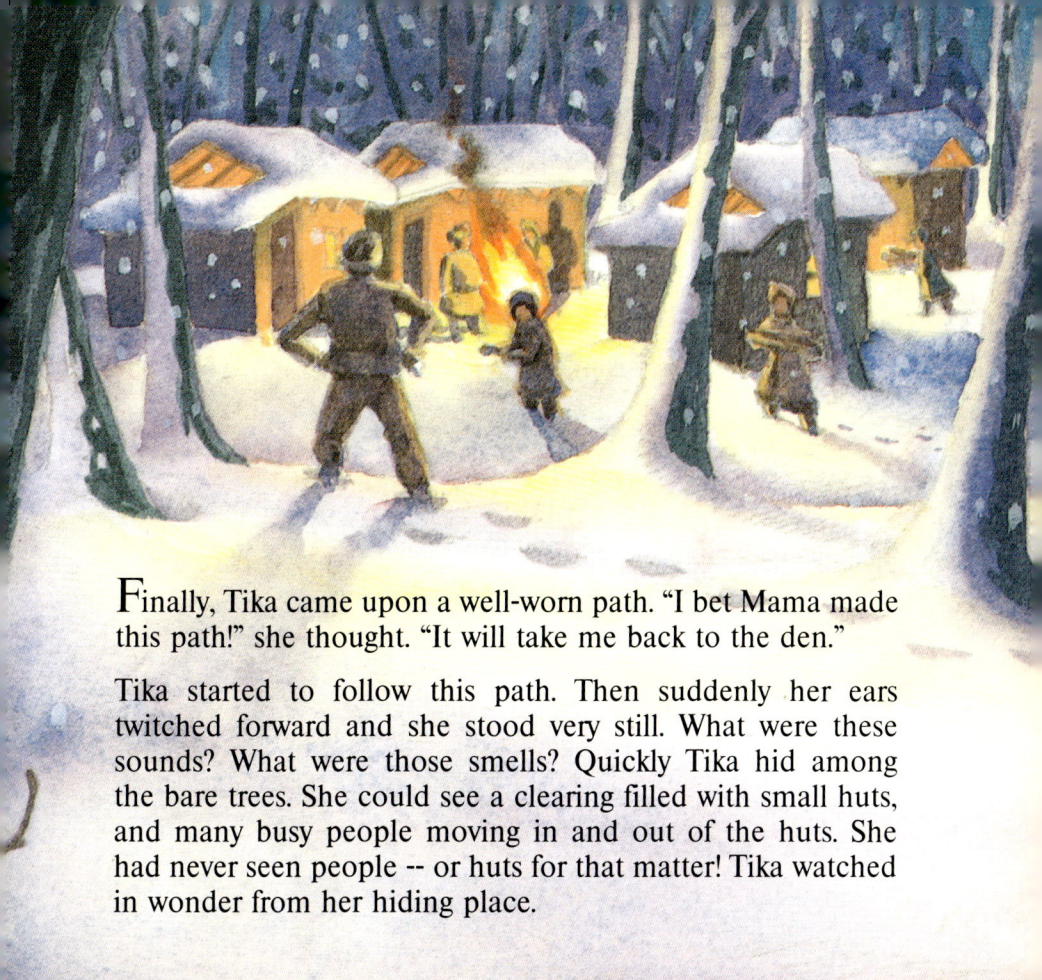

Finally, Tika came upon a well-worn path. "I bet Mama made this path!" she thought. "It will take me back to the den."

Tika started to follow this path. Then suddenly her ears twitched forward and she stood very still. What were these sounds? What were those smells? Quickly Tika hid among the bare trees. She could see a clearing filled with small huts, and many busy people moving in and out of the huts. She had never seen people -- or huts for that matter! Tika watched in wonder from her hiding place.

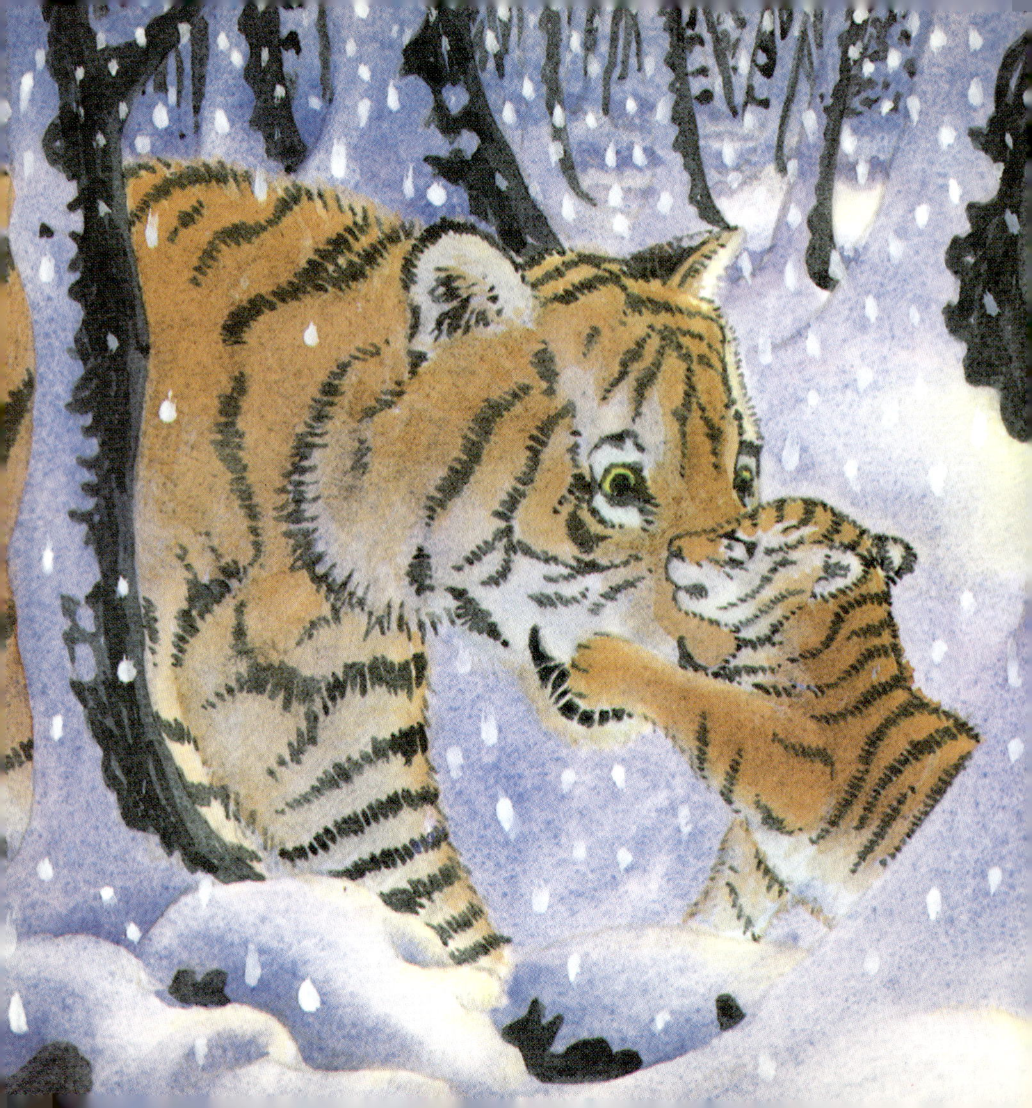

Tika watched the people gather wood, start fires, and prepare their evening meals. The food smelled so good to the hungry little cub, her empty tummy growled. Then suddenly, she was startled by a low voice behind her. Tika turned and saw...

Natasha! Tika's mother had found her! "Mama--" she started to cry out. "Sshh," whispered Natasha.

"Mama," Tika whispered, "I got lost in the forest. I thought I could find my way back to the den, but I just got more and more lost."

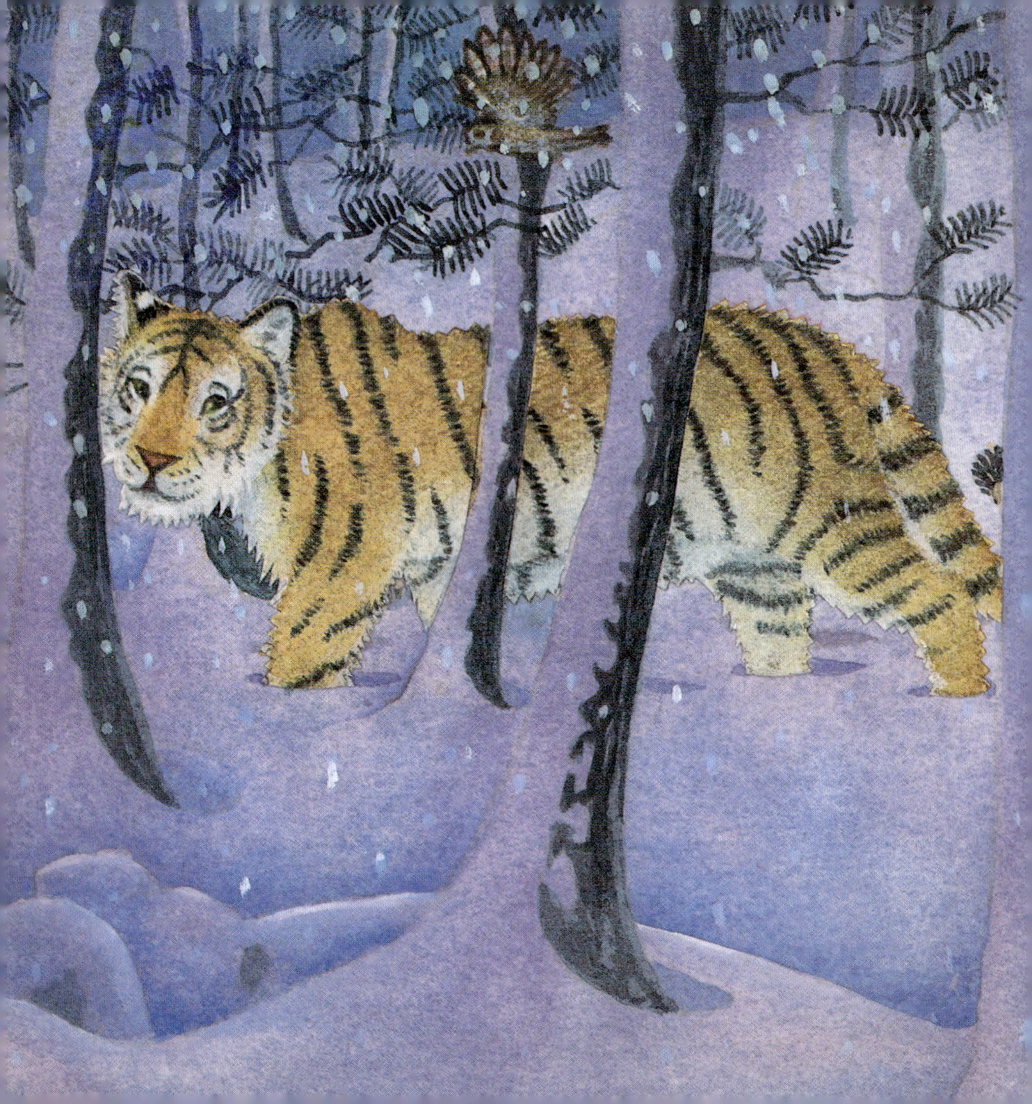

"I know," said Natasha, "I have been following your scent for the past three hours."

Happy Tika and her mother headed for home. The night was very black, but tigers can see well in the dark. "Mama," Tika asked, "who were those creatures back there?"

"We share the forest with many people and many animals," Natasha answered. "Those people are the Udege Indians, and they have lived in these forests for many years. They call us *Amba*, which means Great Monarch. They believe we protect a helpful forest plant called ginseng."

"*Amba*," Tika thought. She liked the sound of it. Soon they came to a small river. Tika was scared. She had never seen a river before. "This is a shortcut," her mother said gently. "You can swim--all tigers can. Just do what I do."

Tika stepped hesitantly into the cold, clear water, following her mother's every move. Soon her feet no longer touched the ground. Tika was swimming as though she had been swimming all her life!

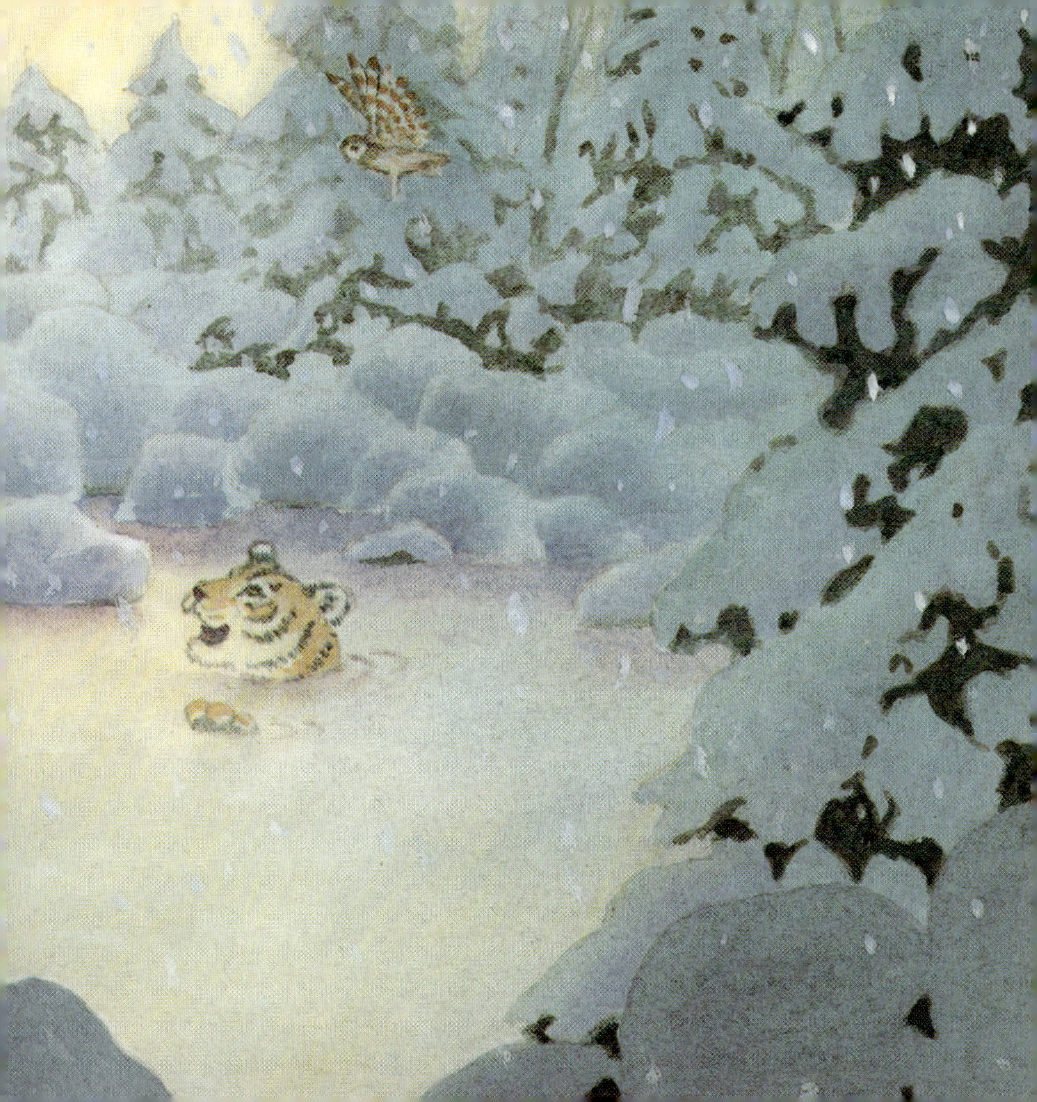

They swam easily to the other bank and shook off the cold water. Then they hurried into the forest, knowing that the den was near.

And there it was! Tika saw the den in the distance. It had never looked so good! But where were Sika and Mika?

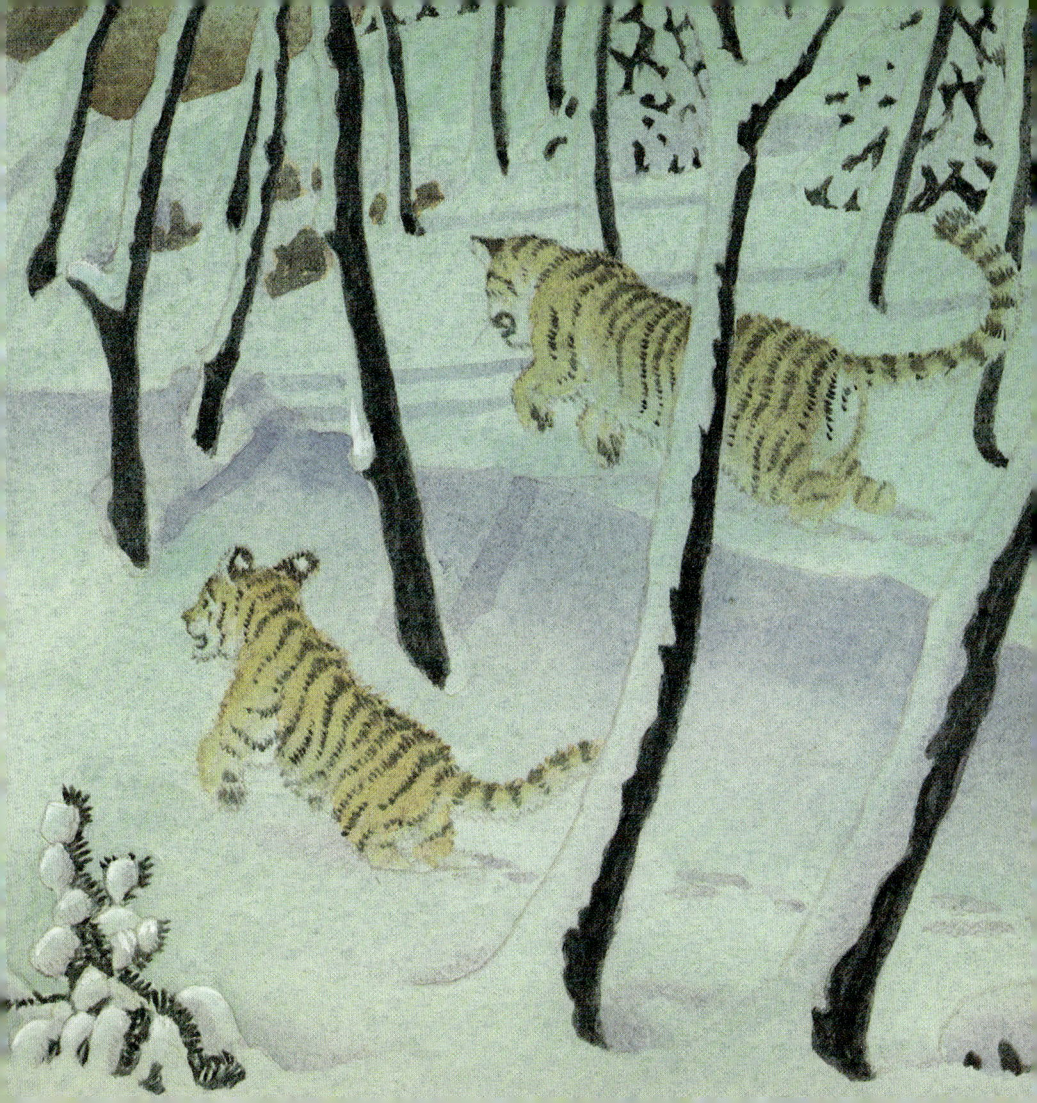

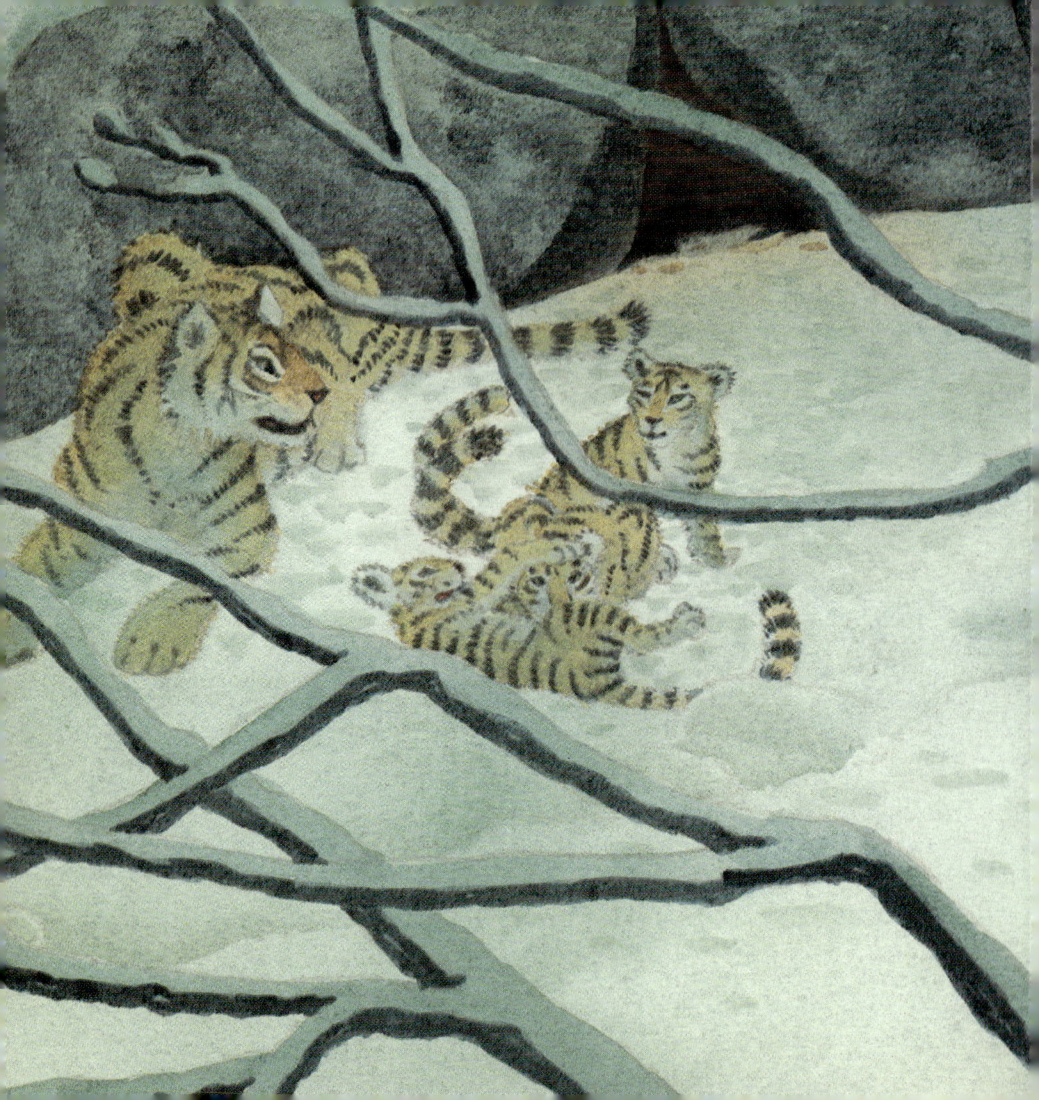

From deep in her throat, Natasha made a low Grrr... sound. Sika and Mika recognized their mother's call, and came bouncing out of the den. "Tika, you're back!" yelled Sika happily. "Tika, you're back!" echoed silly Mika.

The hungry tigers had a lovely dinner with the food that Natasha had hunted. Then the family snuggled together, safe in their cozy den. Natasha licked and groomed her little cubs.

"Tika," her mother said, "Soon I will teach you to know the forest very well. But right now you are too young to be in the forest alone. You must obey me when I tell you to stay in the den."

"Okay, Mama. The forest is exciting. But it's such a big place!" said Tika. "I'll never do that again!"

"Never again..." murmured sleepy Mika.

As the stars twinkled in the clear night sky, Tika drifted off to sleep, curled up snugly with her little tiger family. She dreamed of sparkling rivers and busy villagers. And through her dreams floated a proud and wonderful word: *Amba...*

Tika is a very curious cub. But her mother is right when she says home is the safest place to be. If Tika obeys her mother, she will learn a lot and grow up to be just like her -- a wise, proud Siberian tiger.